VASCO DA GAMA AND THE RISE OF THE PORTUGUESE EMPIRE

COMMANDER GENERAL

Contents

Vasco Da Gama And The Rise Of The Portuguese Empire

COMMANDER GENERAL

v

CHAPTER ONE

INTRODUCTION

The **Portuguese Empire** also known as the **Portuguese Overseas** or the **Portuguese Colonial Empire** was composed of the overseas colonies, factories and the later overseas territories governed by Portugal. It was one of the longest-lived empires in European history, lasting almost six centuries from the conquest of Ceuta in North Africa in 1415 to the transfer of sovereignty over Macau to China in 1999. The empire began in the 15th century and from the early 16th century it stretched across the globe with bases in North and South America, Africa and various regions of Asia and Oceania.

The Portuguese Empire originated at the beginning of the Age of Discovery and the power and influence of the Kingdom of Portugal would eventually expand across the globe. In the wake of the Reconquista, Portuguese sailors began exploring the coast of Africa and the Atlantic archipelagos in 1418–19 using recent developments in navigation, cartography and maritime technology such as the caravel with the aim of finding a sea route to the source of the lucrative spice-trade. In 1488, Bartolomeu Dias rounded the Cape of Good Hope and in 1498 Vasco da Gama reached India. In 1500, either by an accidental landfall or by the crown's secret design, Pedro Álvares Cabral reached what would be Brazil.

Over the following decades, Portuguese sailors continued to explore the coasts and islands of East Asia, establishing forts and trading posts (factories) as they went. By 1571 a string of naval outposts connected Lisbon to Nagasaki along the coasts of Africa, the Middle East, India and South Asia. This commercial network and the colonial trade had a substantial positive impact on Portuguese economic growth (1500–1800) when it accounted for about a fifth of Portugal's per-capita income.

CHAPTER TWO

VASCO DA GAMA

Vasco da Gama (1460 - 1524) was a Portuguese explorer. He led the first expedition that traveled from Europe to India by sailing around Africa.

Vasco da Gama was born in a small coastal town in Portugal named Sines. His father was a knight and an explorer. He followed in his father's footsteps and soon commanded ships in the king's name.

CHAPTER THREE

THE PORTUGUESE EMPIRE

Portugal is a small Western European country at the western tip of the Iberian Peninsula.

Beginning in the 1400s, the Portuguese led by explorers such as Bartolomeu Dias and Vasco da Gama and financed by the great Prince Henry the Navigator sailed to explored and settled in South America, Africa and Asia. Portugal's empire, which survived for more than six centuries was the first of the great European global empires and outlasted all others as well surviving until 1999.

Its former possessions are now across 50 countries around the world.

The Portuguese created colonies for numerous reasons:

- To trade for spices, gold, agricultural products and other resources
- To create more markets for Portuguese goods
- To spread Catholicism
- To "civilize" the natives of these distant places

Portugal's colonies brought great wealth to this small country. But the empire gradually declined as it did for other colonizers, partly because Portugal did not have enough people or resources to maintain so many overseas territories. A move for independence among the colonies finally sealed its fate.

Here are the most important former Portuguese possessions:

Brazil

Brazil was by far Portugal's largest colony by area and population. It was reached by the Portuguese in 1500 and was part of the Treaty of Tordesillas signed with Spain in 1494 allowing Portugal claim over Brazil. The Portuguese imported enslaved Africans and forced them to grow sugar, tobacco, cotton, coffee and other cash crops.

The Portuguese also extracted brazilwood from the rainforest, which was used to dye European textiles. They also helped to explore and settle the vast interior of Brazil.

In the 19th century, the royal court of Portugal lived in and governed both Portugal and Brazil from Rio de Janeiro. Brazil gained independence from Portugal in 1822.

Angola, Mozambique and Guinea-Bissau

In the 1500s, Portugal colonized the present-day west African country of Guinea-Bissau and the two southern African countries of Angola and Mozambique.

The Portuguese captured and enslaved many people from these countries and sent them to the New World. Gold and diamonds were also extracted from these colonies.

In the 20th century, Portugal was under international pressure to release its colonies, but Portugal's dictator

Antonio Salazar refused to decolonize.

Several independence movements in these three African countries erupted into the Portuguese Colonial War of the 1960s and 1970s, which killed tens of thousands and was associated with communism and the Cold War.

In 1974, a military coup in Portugal forced Salazar out of power and the new government of Portugal ended the unpopular and expensive war. Angola, Mozambique and Guinea-Bissau gained independence in 1975.

All three countries were underdeveloped and civil wars in the decades after independence took millions of lives. More than a million refugees from these three countries emigrated to Portugal after independence and strained the Portuguese economy.

Cape Verde and Sao Tome and Principe

Cape Verde and Sao Tome and Principe, two small archipelagos located off the western coast of Africa were also colonized by the Portuguese. (Sao Tome and Principe are two small islands making up a single country.)

They were uninhabited before the Portuguese arrived and were used in the slave trade. They both achieved independence from Portugal in 1975.

Goa, India

In the 1500s, the Portuguese colonized the western Indian region of Goa. Goa, located on the Arabian Sea was an important port in spice-rich India. In 1961, India annexed Goa from the Portuguese and it became an Indian state. Goa has many Catholic adherents in primarily Hindu India.

East Timor

The Portuguese also colonized the eastern half of the island of Timor in the 16th century. In 1975, East Timor declared independence from Portugal, but the island was invaded and annexed by Indonesia. East Timor became independent in 2002.

Macau

In the 16th century, the Portuguese colonized Macau on the South China Sea. Macau served as an important Southeast Asian trading port. The Portuguese empire ended when Portugal handed over control of Macau to China in 1999.

PORTUGUESE LANGUAGE

Portuguese, a Romance language is spoken by 260 million people with between 215 million and 220 million native speakers. It is the sixth most spoken language in the world.

It is the official language of Portugal, Brazil, Angola, Mozambique, Guinea-Bissau, Cape Verde, Sao Tome and Principe and East Timor. It is also spoken in Macau and Goa.

It is one of the official languages of the European Union, the African Union and the Organization of American States. Brazil, with more than 207 million people (July 2017 estimate), is the most populated Portuguese-speaking country in the world.

Portuguese is also spoken in the Azores Islands and the Madeira Islands, two archipelagos that still belong to Portugal.

CHAPTER FIVE

CONCLUSION

The Portuguese excelled in exploration and trade for centuries. The country's former colonies, spread across continents, have varying areas, populations, geographies, histories and cultures.

The Portuguese tremendously affected their colonies politically, economically and socially. The empire has been criticized for being exploitative, neglectful and racist.

Some colonies still suffer from high poverty and instability, but their valuable natural resources, combined with current diplomatic relations with and assistance from Portugal, may improve the living conditions of these numerous countries.

The Portuguese language will always be an important connector of these countries and a reminder of how vast and significant the Portuguese empire once was.

www.ingramcontent.com/pod-product-compliance
Lightning Source LLC
Chambersburg PA
CBHW032018140726
47988CB00018B/1725